Financial Freedom Through Frugal Living

A Comprehensive Guide

Table of Contents

Chapter 1. Introduction

Welcome to your journey to financial independence! "Financial Freedom Through Frugal Living: A Comprehensive Guide" is an enticing Special Report that will inspire you to achieve what once felt like an unobtainable dream. This isn't about leading a joyless life, pinching pennies at every corner. Instead, it invites you to reassess your relationship with money, to truly understand its value, and to celebrate the idea of living more with less. Imagine the peace of mind achieved by attaining financial security, not through a sudden windfall or a high paying job, but through the conscious decisions you make every day. Let's embark on this journey together, where financial freedom is not just a far-off destination, but a fulfilling journey achieved through mindful, frugal living. So ready to revolutionize your life and pockets? Your key to financial freedom is just a purchase away!

Chapter 2. The Essence of Frugal Living

Frugal living is not simply a method of budgeting or a basic set of habits; it's a philosophy of life. At its core, frugality is about making intentional choices to conserve resources and prioritize long-term goals over short-term desires. Often, it's a journey of self-discovery, self-improvement, and fulfillment.

2.1. The Philosophy of Frugality

The culture we live in often prompts us to believe that comfort, happiness, and even personal identity are obtained through consumption. Frugality challenges this belief. It preaches that value doesn't rest in what we own, but in what we do, what we know, the relationships we foster, and the experiences we cultivate.

Frugality is a philosophy that encourages us to be smart and strategic about how we utilize our resources. It nudges us to be wise consumers, investing in goods and experiences that provide authentic, long-lasting satisfaction rather than temporary materialism.

It's not about depriving oneself but rather about optimal usage of money and other resources. It is about determining what truly brings us satisfaction, joy, and long-term benefit, and then aligning our spending habits with these values.

2.2. Living within Your Means, Not Your Desires

Living frugally does not mean mandating a Spartan lifestyle. Instead, it is about understanding the difference between wants and needs, between instant gratification and lasting satisfaction. It's about acknowledging the simple truth that you cannot have everything you want, but you can have the things that really matter to you.

Living within your means requires you to establish clear financial priorities and make economic decisions that align with these. It might mean foregoing the newest iPhone to save for a much-needed family holiday. It may mean choosing to brew your coffee at home rather than buying from a pricey café every day, allowing you to invest more in your retirement.

Frugality teaches the benefit of contentment. It cultivates an appreciation for what we have rather than a constant yearning for what we do not possess.

2.3. Planning and Budgeting

The crux of frugality is effective financial planning and budgeting. The more detailed your plan, the clearer your financial picture will be, allowing you to make informed decisions and locate areas where you can increase efficiency and reduce waste.

Establish clear, measurable, attainable, results-focused, and time-bound financial goals. This method, known as the SMART system, can revolutionize how you manage your financial resources.

Budgeting should be an integral part of this process. A well-structured budget permits prioritization of needs over wants, allowing you to live within your means.

Certain free tools, like budgeting apps, can ease this process, offering insights into your spending habits and where your money is going.

2.4. The Impact of Small Choices

One of the fundamental principles of frugal living is understanding the cumulative impact of small choices. That disposable coffee cup you buy each day, while seemingly insignificant on its own, can add up to a substantial sum over time.

Start to question each expense: is it necessary? Is it offering value for money? How does it match your long-term financial goals? Understanding and keeping track of these daily decisions is essential to fostering a mindset that recognizes the influence of small choices on substantial financial outcomes.

2.5. Frugal Living and the Environment

An often-overlooked benefit of frugal living is the positive impact it has on the environment. Our spending habits directly influence the demand for goods. By choosing to consume less or selecting environmentally-friendly alternatives, we can help reduce the demand for products that harm the environment.

Frugality champions the principles of waste reduction, reuse, and recycling to make the most out of what we have. A reward of this is its contribution to environmental preservation.

2.6. Gratitude and Mindfulness

Frugality involves an element of mindfulness, a form of consciousness about our actions and decisions, especially regarding our resource use. It encourages a stop-and-think approach, assessing whether a decision aligns with our underlying value system and long-term goals before acting.

Gratitude links closely with this. By taking the time to appreciate what we have, we can limit the desire for constant acquisition. Living frugally provides for a more intentional, conscious, and ultimately satisfying lifestyle, rendering us happier in the long run.

Time-tested and centred on timeless values, frugal living can offer both financial independence and genuine satisfaction, not through what we acquire, but through the joy of living a purpose-filled life. Fortunately, frugality is accessible to anyone willing to rethink their relationship with money and develop a strategic approach to their savings and spending habits. It doesn't involve winning the lottery or scoring a six-figure job; it's about the small, intentional choices we make every day that move us closer to our financial goals.

Chapter 3. Understanding Your Relationship with Money

To truly march towards financial independence through frugal living, it is paramount that we first dissect and comprehend our relationship with money. An intertwined mesh of social conditioning, personal experiences, and innate tendencies; our relationship with money helps shape our financial behaviors and their consequent outcomes.

3.1. The Psychological Aspect of Money

The first step on this journey is to acknowledge that our financial decisions are not solely driven by numerical logic. They are deeply rooted in our psyche. Money, in essence, is not just a medium of exchange — it represents power, security, and freedom, while simultaneously invoking emotions of fear, stress, and even guilt. Understanding these emotional underpinnings can provide us with valuable insights into our money habits.

A framework developed by psychologist Dr. Kathleen Gurney called the Nine Money Personalities has been instrumental in this context. These personalities — hoarder, spender, money monk, avoider, and amasser, to name a few — reflect our emotions, behaviors, and attitudes towards money.

For instance, a hoarder, driven by security, may find it hard to part with any amount of money, while a spender is likely to derive pleasure and instant gratification from purchases. Recognizing and accepting these tendencies is the first step towards reshaping our money habits.

3.2. Social and Cultural Conditioning

Humans are innately social creatures, and our upbringing and society significantly impact our outlook towards money. In certain societies, high consumption and ostentatious display of wealth are seen as signs of success, while others may value thrift, frugality, and savings.

Assessing and acknowledging the effects of social conditioning on our financial behaviors is a critical step in redefining our relationship with money. A simple exercise could be listing out our top money beliefs and evaluating whether they are our own or learned from family, friends, or society.

3.3. Assessing Personal Experiences

Our personal experiences with money, particularly in our early years, tend to leave lasting impressions. For instance, if one grew up in a household where there was consistent financial instability, security might be valued over the risky pursuit of wealth. On the contrary, growing up in affluence may either lead to a similar need for comfort or a desire to establish self-sufficiency.

Reflecting on these experiences will assist in recognizing the patterns that impact our current financial behaviors and aid in charting a path towards better money management.

3.4. Money and Self-worth

Money's intricacy weaves beyond just the functions of buying and saving; it often braids itself with our sense of self-worth. Individuals can assess their value based on their income, net worth, possessions, or residual debt. This intertwining can lead to adverse impacts on our financial decisions and overall mental health. Recognizing this association and understanding that self-worth is not synonymous with net worth is a monumental step towards a healthier relationship with money.

3.5. Financial Fear and Anxiety

The lack of financial literacy, coupled with the uncertainty surrounding money matters, can trigger fear and anxiety. From investing in stocks to filing taxes, the financial world can often seem daunting. By actively seeking knowledge and skills, these challenges can be subdued. Confronting our fears and educating ourselves financially cannot be stressed enough. Knowledge, in this scenario, indeed, serves as power.

3.6. Money Mindset and Attitudes

Our money mindset encompasses our overall perspective about money and how we associate it with our lives. It can be broadly categorized into scarcity (money as a finite resource) or abundance (unlimited potential to earn).

Cultivating a mindset is not about ignoring the reality of financial constraints. It is about harboring a positive attitude while making sensible decisions. This shift in mindset might be just the catalyst needed for your financial evolution.

In conclusion, understanding our relationship with money becomes the foundation for financial freedom. Unravel the intertwined mesh, step back, evaluate, understand, and consciously rewire your relationship with money. As you navigate through this path, always remember that money is not an end but a means to the end. And that end is the freedom to lead the life you envision for yourself. It's not just about saving more, but about living better, aware of your financial reality but not bound by it. Let's begin this journey towards financial freedom with self-awareness, comprehension, acceptance, and ample compassion towards ourselves in our financial pursuits.

Chapter 4. Strategies for Effective Budgeting

Every financial independence journey begins with a practical grasp on how to effectively budget. It is a fundamental skill necessary for successfully managing personal finances. By implementing strategic budgeting, you force yourself to be more conscious of your financial habits, providing you with a clear vision for your future. Effective budgeting is not about limiting your spending but instead about understanding where your money goes and making purposeful decisions.

4.1. Understanding Your Current Spending Habits

Before you begin creating a budget, evaluate your current spending habits. This step is crucial as it provides the baseline for your budget plan. Start by gathering your financial documents like bank statements, credit card bills, utility bills, and any other recurring expenses. Once you have all these documents, categorize your spendings like groceries, utilities, entertainment, rent, and so on. There are several asciidoc templates one can use to efficiently sort out this information.

For example:

```
Expenses Category | Amount ($)
------------------|-----------
Groceries | 200
Rent | 1000
Utilities | 150
Entertainment | 100
```

This detailed study of your expenditure will highlight where your disposable income is going. This exercise also provides an opportunity to recognize unnecessary expenses and eliminate them.

4.2. Identifying Your Financial Goals

Next, outline your financial goals- be it saving for a down payment on a house, paying off a credit card debt, or achieving financial freedom. It's important to have both short term and long term goals as it helps you stay focused and motivated. Segregate your goals into small actionable steps, making them feel attainable.

For example:

```
Short-term Goals | Long-term Goals
-----------------|-----------------
Emergency Fund for six months | Clear credit card debt
Save for a vacation | Retirement savings
```

4.3. Drafting the Budget

With your spending habits examined and your financial goals identified, it's time to draft your budget. Here your aim should be to outline a spending plan that ensures your income covers your monthly expenditure and also contributes towards your savings or debt reduction goals.

Again, the asciidoc table format may be used: --- Income | Expenditure | Savings/Debt Reduction ----------|---------------- |------------------------- 3000 | 2000 | 1000 ---

In drafting the budget, remember to follow the 50/30/20 rule that recommends dedicating 50% of your income to necessities, 30% to wants, and 20% to savings or debt repayments.

4.4. Adjusting Your Budget Over Time

Budgeting is a dynamic process. You'll often find the need to make adjustments and accommodate for unexpected expenses or fluctuations in income. Regularly revisiting your budget helps be aware of changes and lets you make necessary modifications sooner.

4.5. Automating Savings

Once you've got your budget set up, consider automating your savings and bill payments. It ensures routine payments and transfers are done without the need for your intervention and diminishes the risk of forgetting a payment.

4.6. Implementing the Zero-Based Budget

The zero-based budget is a method that assigns every dollar a role. It ensures that the income minus the outgo equals zero. This system could be efficient for controlling your money and making every dollar work for you.

In conclusion, effective budgeting can seem daunting but remember that it is an ongoing process, requiring regular adjustments and revisions. Trust the process and you're essentially moving a step closer to gaining control over your financial future.

Chapter 5. Practical Money-Saving Techniques

Everyday Savings

Saving money begins with mindfulness. It's about knowing where every penny goes, understanding why it goes there, and making purposeful decisions about its trajectory. Indeed, each day presents numerous opportunities to save.

5.1. The 30-Day Rule

A major hurdle in achieving financial freedom is rampant consumerism. Impulse purchases can empty your pockets faster than you'd like. To combat this, adopt the '30-Day rule'. When you find an item you want to buy, wait 30 days before making the purchase. This gives you the time to evaluate whether it's a need or a want. You'd be surprised to find how many times the impulse wears off, saving you from frivolous purchases.

5.2. The Thrift Habit

Thrift stores are often treasure troves. Buying second-hand items is not just advantageous from a financial aspect, but it's ethical too. From clothes to books, home décor to appliances, thrifting can drastically reduce expenditure. It might take a little getting used to, but the savings more than makeup for it.

Do It Yourself

Taking matters into your own hands not just saves money, but it also equips you with valuable skills and a sense of fulfillment.

5.3. Home Cooking

Rather than dining out or ordering delivery, make a conscious effort to prepare meals at home. Not only is this healthier, you have control over your ingredients, portions, and costs. To make the process easier, consider meal planning and bulk cooking.

5.4. Home Maintenance

A little bit of knowledge and a set of tools can prevent many minor issues from blossoming into expensive repairs. Learn to fix minor leaks, unclog drains, or patch walls. When something breaks, instead of replacing it outright, see if it can be fixed.

5.5. DIY Gifts

Creating gifts yourself gives them a personal touch, and is a definite saving method. Homemade soaps, custom artworks - the possibilities are limitless!

Investing in Efficiency

Sometimes, it pays to spend a little more upfront for long-term savings.

5.6. Energy Efficiency

Switch to energy-saving appliances and light bulbs, have a smart thermostat, or install a solar panel for sustainable energy. While these represent an initial investment, their long-term savings are substantial.

5.7. Quality Over Quantity

When buying any items, choose quality over quantity. A quality product might cost more initially, but its longevity will often save you money in the long run.

Budgeting and Tracking

Without tracking, saving can seem like a daunting task. But with the right tools, it can become an exciting game.

5.8. Needs Versus Wants

Make a habit of distinguishing between needs and wants. Rent, groceries, utility bills, these are needs. Concert tickets, designer handbags, the latest videogames- these are wants. Be honest with yourself, and you are halfway to understanding where you can make cutbacks.

5.9. Budget Planning

Create a budget, preferably on a monthly basis. List your income sources, necessary expenditures, and ascertain how much you can afford to save.

5.10. Financial Goals

Have clear financial goals. It's motivating to have a target to reach and can greatly help you stay on track.

5.11. The Envelope System

Consider using the envelope system, where cash for every category of expenditure is kept in separate envelopes. When an envelope is empty, you cannot spend anymore from that category. This physical, visual limitation is effective in managing overspending.

5.12. Discount Hunting

Coupons, sales, seasonal pricing, student and senior discounts can add up significantly. Be on the lookout for these opportunities.

5.13. Mobile Apps and Tools

Numerous tools can help you visualize, track, and manage your savings. Mint, YNAB (You Need A Budget), and PocketGuard are just a couple of them.

Remember, leading a frugal life doesn't mean leading a joyless life. The journey to financial freedom is as fulfilling as the destination. Should you falter, do not give up. It's a marathon, not a sprint, and every penny saved is a penny earned.

Chapter 6. Living Well on Less: A Deep Dive

The concept of frugal living has sometimes received a bad rep, unfairly associated with a lifestyle devoid of pleasure, comfort, or contentment. This couldn't be farther from the truth. Frugality is not about miserly behavior; rather, it's about optimizing the use of available resources in a manner that enhances life's quality whilst minimizing wastage. Living well on less might seem a daunting proposition initially. However, once we dive into its intricacies, every aspect—from grocery shopping to weekend entertainment—turns into an opportunity to celebrate simplicity, thriftiness, and sustainable living.

6.1. Understanding What Frugality Means

To many, the term 'frugality' sounds somewhat negative—indicative of bleak, spartan lifestyles. However, true frugality is a matter of selective spending rather than scarcity. It's about prioritizing your expenditures according to what truly matters to you, and judiciously avoiding unnecessary expense otherwise.

Don't equate a frugal lifestyle with deprivation. It is meant to liberate you from the shackles of unhealthy consumerism, enabling you to enjoy a higher quality of life, not marred by financial stress and pressures.

6.2. Cultivating the Frugal Mindset

Adopting a frugal lifestyle requires cultivating a 'frugal mindset'. This doesn't mean blindly cutting corners everywhere. Instead, it's about examining resource utilization and systematically eliminating waste. At its core, a frugal mindset means being resourceful, flexible, and considerate about consumption patterns.

Understand the difference between needs and wants. Pursue simplicity and make everyday life an opportunity to save, not to surrender to the consumerist culture that encourages spendthrift and wasteful behavior.

6.3. Reducing Housing Costs

For most individuals, housing costs tend to be the largest line item in the monthly budget. Therefore, managing these costs effectively has a substantial impact on your overall financial picture.

Live within your means. Consider downsizing if your current living situation is more extensive than necessary. Consider a roommate to share expenses if your living situation allows. Also, reconsider your geographic location: living in high-cost metropolitan areas may seem appealing, but often, relocating to a lower-cost area can provide a significant boost to your savings without compromising quality of life.

6.4. Saving on Food Expenditure

Large-scale food wastage is a global issue. Not only is it ethically questionable, but it also has a significant financial impact on a personal level. Plan your meals, ensure effective grocery shopping, and manage leftovers wisely.

Cook more, and dine out less. Home-cooking saves massively while putting your health in your own hands. Buying in bulk from wholesale markets, growing your own vegetables, and learning to conserve and creatively use leftovers can lead to substantial savings.

6.5. Being Mindful about Energy Usage

Energy conservation benefits both the environment and your wallet. Switch off electrical appliances when not in use, use energy-efficient light sources like LEDs, and utilize natural sunlight and ventilation as much as possible. Some initial investment in an energy-efficient home setup can lead to consistent long-term savings.

6.6. Choosing Economical Modes of Transport

Transportation costs can also contribute significantly to your monthly expenditure. Choose the most economical mode of transport for your routine—public transit, cycling, carpooling, or walking. The added benefit is reducing your environmental footprint and potentially improving your health.

6.7. Investing Wisely

Smart investing is essential in a frugal lifestyle. Money saved should be not left unused but invested wisely to work for you, creating additional income streams. Investing may sound intimidating, but with the plethora of resources available, anyone can learn to be a smart investor. Don't shy away from seeking professional advice if needed.

6.8. Remembering to Enjoy Life

Frugality is not about leading a life devoid of joy but about finding happiness outside excess. There is considerably more enjoyment to life than what money can buy. Build relationships not with things, but with people. Pursue hobbies and interests that genuinely make you happy.

By implementing these ideas, you'll be steadily marching towards financial freedom, enjoying a lifestyle that places value on the important things—people, experiences, and peace of mind. Remember, the frugal journey is exhilarating and fulfilling in its own right. More than reaching a destination, it's about the simple enjoyment of the journey there.

Chapter 7. Cutting Corners without Cutting Out Joy

Let's dive deep into the heart of frugality: strategic spending. This doesn't mean you eliminate all joy and happiness from your life to save each and every penny. Instead, you can lead a fulfilling, content life without compromising your financial goals. One of the wonders of this financial journey is learning how we can cut corners without cutting out joy. Let's explore this in detail.

7.1. The Philosophy of Frugality

Frugality is not about scarcity or depriving yourself. It is about aligning your spending with what truly makes you happy. Often, we spend money without actually deriving happiness from the purchase. To truly embody the philosophy of frugality, we must understand where our money goes and whether those expenditures truly enrich our lives.

7.2. Mindful Consumption

One of the most effective tools for frugal living is mindful consumption. Make the conscious effort to consider each purchase carefully before you make it. Ask yourself: 'Do I really need this? Will this purchase significantly improve my life?' Often, we end up buying things out of habit, without really evaluating their purpose or necessity in our lives. By practicing mindful consumption, you not only save money but also decrease clutter in your home.

7.3. Strategically Spend, Don't Splurge

Find joy in strategic spending. Instead of buying a daily coffee, invest in a good coffee machine and enjoy high-quality coffee at home. Rather than eating out frequently, spend time and effort to build your cooking skills. This doesn't mean you banish all fun from your life. Instead of an expensive movie night out, you could enjoy a movie night at home with home-cooked popcorn. You'll find more fulfillment in these activities as they not just save money but also help in honing your skills and spending quality time with your loved ones.

7.4. DIY: A Frugal Superpower

Do-It-Yourself (DIY) skills are a superpower in the realm of frugality. With numerous online resources available today, you can pick up several handy skills. From home repairs to knitting your own clothes to growing your vegetables, DIY skills can save you tons of money. Plus, the feeling of accomplishment and self-reliance that comes from gaining a new skill is priceless!

7.5. Luxurious Frugality

Embracing frugality doesn't mean you have to lead a sparse, joyless life. On the contrary, you can find luxury and abundance in the small, everyday things. Enjoy a luxurious home-cooked meal, immerse yourself in a good book, take a relaxing bath, or practice yoga. None of these activities require a lot of spending, but they can bring immense joy and peace.

7.6. Patience: A Key Ingredient

An essential trait in frugal living is patience. We're often tempted by instant gratification, but that's not the most frugal way. Whether it's waiting for a sale, or not upgrading your phone as soon as a new model comes out, patience can lead to substantial savings.

7.7. Spending Less on Essentials

Consider cutting costs on essentials. Simple actions, like turning off lights when leaving a room, can lead to notable savings on utilities. When buying groceries, opt for store brands instead of name brands, they often offer the same quality at a fraction of the cost.

7.8. Celebrating for Less

Who says celebrations need to be expensive? Small, intimate gatherings with loved ones are usually more memorable than extravagant parties. DIY gifts are unique, personal, and cost-effective. Creating a tradition around affordable or free activities can bring joy and create priceless memories.

Remember, frugality is not a chore or a punishment, but an opportunity to reassess your values, to find joy and happiness in mindful consumption, and to grow both financially and personally. You'll be amazed at all the corners you can cut without cutting out joy, and the amount of money you can save in the process.

Chapter 8. Investing Wisely with Savings

The word "investing" can often seem daunting - an activity left solely to the financial wizards on Wall Street. Ironically, society's detached view of investing may deter us from realizing its essential role in accomplishing financial freedom. Through incremental savings and astute investment, your money can become a powerful tool, generating passive income and growing your overall wealth.

8.1. Understanding the Power of Saving

"The best time to plant a tree was 20 years ago. The second best time is now." – Chinese Proverb

The earlier you start saving, the more your money can grow, thanks to the magic of compound interest. Compound interest refers to the method of calculating interest where the interest gained over time is added to the original amount, and the interest for the future is calculated on this increased value. This process helps your savings grow at a much faster rate.

Consider this: if you saved $500 a month from the age of 25, assuming an annual interest rate of 5%, you would have accumulated approximately $822,000 by the time you reach 65. In contrast, if you started saving the same amount at 35 years old with the same interest rate, you'd have approximately $488,000. That decade of delay could cost you nearly $334,000!

Therefore, start saving early. Set aside at least 10-15% of your income every month. Even small amounts add up over time, especially when interest is considered.

8.2. Investing Your Savings Wisely

Now that you're saving, the primary goal should be to preserve and grow your financial assets. It's not just about keeping money safe in a bank account; it's about growing those funds by investing wisely. Here's how:

1. **Understand Your Risk Tolerance:** First, identify how much risk you're willing to take on. Enterprise and government bonds are low-risk, providing stable, albeit lower returns. Stocks, on the other hand, are riskier but can offer significant returns. Determine your comfort zone.

2. **Diversify:** Don't put all your eggs in one basket. Diversify your portfolio across various asset classes like stocks, bonds, real estate, and others. Even within an asset class, spread your investments – for instance, invest in stocks across different industries. This will mitigate the risk of a single investment failing.

3. **Consistency:** Steady, regular investments often fare better than sporadic, large ones. The practice of investing a fixed amount regularly, irrespective of market conditions, is called dollar-cost averaging. This strategy eliminates the need to time the market and reduces the impact of market volatility on your investment.

4. **Education:** Stay updated on investment trends and news. Remember, knowledge is power – By educating yourself, you're arming yourself with the best tool to make informed financial decisions.

8.3. Building Your Investment Strategy

Once you understand the fundamentals, it's time to construct your investment plan. While it might seem intimidating, by breaking it down into manageable steps, even beginners can navigate the investment landscape effectively.

1. **Set Your Goals:** Be clear on why you're investing. Is it for retirement, your children's education, a new house, or something else? Having clear goals will drive your investment strategy, define your risk tolerance, and determine your time horizon.

2. **Choose the Right Investment Plan:** Based on your goals, risk tolerance, and investment period, choose the right investment vehicles. An investment with higher short-term volatility (like stocks) might be suitable for long-term goals, whereas immediate goals require more stable investments (like bonds or money markets).

3. **Monitor Your Investments:** Regularly review and adjust your investment portfolio. Your risk tolerance, financial situation, and investment goals may change over time. Ensure your investment portfolio aligns with these evolutions.

4. **Consider Professional Help:** If you're unsure, consider reaching out to a financial advisor who can provide guidance and manage your investments. Ensure to choose an advisor who has your best interest at heart.

8.4. Saving and Investing — A Symbiotic Relationship

Saving and investing, although different, work synchronously in achieving your financial independence. Saving helps you accumulate wealth gradually while investing propels that wealth to grow exponentially. Remember, being frugal and wise with your finances is a lifestyle choice and one that leads you to the prosperous path of financial freedom. Your journey to financial independence commences with the first penny saved and first cent invested. The road to wealth is long, and the destination may seem far away, but with every step forward, you're inching closer to your goal. Let the journey of saving aggressively and investing wisely begin!

Chapter 9. Navigating Common Spending Traps

The path to financial freedom is fraught with myriad obstacles designed to deter you from your goal. These pitfalls, often couched as 'unavoidable expenses' or 'necessary splurges,' reliably siphon away your hard-earned money, leaving you compromised. The first step towards averting this drain is to understand and identify these common spending traps.

9.1. Recognizing Unnecessary Spending

Understanding the distinction between a need and a want is pivotal to financial independence. Needs are expenses that are absolutely necessary for survival like food, rent or mortgage payments, utilities, and healthcare. Wants, on the other hand, are not essential to survival but tend to make life more enjoyable or comfortable.

Inspect your monthly budget and expenditures to gain clarity on where your money goes. This involves scrutinizing your spendings in light of 'need or want.' Small, seemingly innocuous purchases can add up over time, effectively becoming a spending trap. Meanwhile, expensive one-off buys present an immediate threat to your financial stability.

9.2. Mindless Shopping

Many people fall into the trap of mindless shopping, buying items unaligned to their needs or goals. Reasons include sales and discounts, shopping as a pastime, or succumbing to impulse purchases. Although shopping can provide momentary satisfaction, it can also lead to "buyer's remorse" or serious financial implications in the long run.

Mitigating this requires mindfulness. Ask yourself 'Do I need this?' before each purchase. Consider the real utility and validity of new acquisitions. Prioritize needs over wants, and ensure that all your purchases align with your long-term financial goals.

9.3. High Interest Debt

High interest rate debt, particularly from credit cards or personal loans, is another common spending trap. These debts can quickly snowball if not managed efficiently, leaving you mired in ongoing payments.

Start by understanding all the loans you owe and their corresponding interest rates. Focus on paying off the highest interest debts first while making minimum required payments on the remaining. Also, resist the temptation to use credit cards for non-emergencies, and try to always pay off the balance in full each month.

9.4. Overspending on Housing

Housing can sink your budget if not carefully considered. The conventional financial wisdom posits that housing should not consume more than 30% of your income. In urban areas with high cost of living, adhering to this benchmark can be challenging, but it prevents you from finding yourself 'house poor,' unable to afford life outside of your housing payments.

Find ways to offset your housing costs. Consider a smaller home or apartment, negotiate rent or mortgage rates, and if possible, take on a roommate.

9.5. Overpriced Convenience

Convenience often comes at an inflated price. Prepared meals, ride-sharing services, or delivery services are attractive and easy, but their costs add up. By preparing meals at home, using public transportation, and limiting use of convenience services, substantial savings can be realized.

9.6. Extravagant Vacations

While it's important to enjoy life and take breaks, extravagant vacations can cripple your budget. Aim for modest, well-planned vacations. Look for off-peak deals, discounts, and consider enjoying local attractions.

9.7. Miscellaneous & Hidden Costs

Unexpected and hidden costs can skew your planned budget. Always keep some funding aside for miscellaneous expenses and exercise due diligence, especially before committing to long-term contracts.

In conclusion, financial freedom ultimately comes down to conscious money management. Avoiding the common spending traps means making intentional, proactive choices about how and where you spend your money. Informed, careful decision-making, coupled with a steady stream of discipline, can be the difference between perpetual money stress and the peace that accompanies financial independence.

Chapter 10. The Roadmap to Financial Freedom

Before we set foot on this exciting journey, it's important to understand what financial freedom actually means. It isn't about living a life of opulence and extravagance, but rather, achieving a state where earning money is an option, not a necessity. It means having your income resources - savings, investments, passive income generators, cover your expenses. So, how can you attain this seemingly elusive state? Let's dive in.

10.1. Understanding Your Money

The cornerstone to creating your financial roadmap is a thorough understanding of your money, its sources, its uses, and its potential for growth.

First, consider your income. This might be from a single source, like a regular job, or from multiple streams like part-time work, stock dividends, or rental income. Having multiple income sources is a great way to boost financial resilience.

Next, map your expenses. Separate your essential needs from your wants. Essential needs include fixed costs like rent, utility bills, and groceries. The variable costs include discretionary expenses on non-essentials like eating out, entertainment, gadgets, and vacations.

Once you have a clear picture of your income and expense, identify potential areas for savings by cutting unnecessary spending or increasing your income. The key here isn't to eliminate enjoyment from life but to ensure that every dollar spent provides value to you.

10.2. Establishing Your Financial Goals

Whether it's paying off debt, saving for a house, investing for retirement, or being able to live on passive income, your financial goals will guide your path to achieving financial freedom. Outline both your short-term goals (achievable within a year), medium-term goals (achievable within five years), and long-term goals (achievable within ten years or more). Make your goals SMART, that is, Specific, Measurable, Achievable, Relevant, and Time-bound.

10.3. Implementing a Budget

A budget is essentially a finance plan for your money. It aligns your income with your savings and expenses, setting clear boundaries for each category. To aid in this, you can use the '50/30/20' rule. According to this rule, you allocate 50% of your income towards needs, 30% towards wants, and the remaining 20% towards savings. However, you can adjust these percentages according to your lifestyle and financial goals.

10.4. Building an Emergency Fund

Having an emergency fund is like having a financial buffer against unexpected expenses like medical emergencies, vehicle repairs, or sudden job loss. Ideally, your emergency fund should cover three to six months' worth of living expenses. Although it may take a while to save up, this fund is a crucial step towards achieving financial freedom.

10.5. Eliminating Debt

Debt can be a significant obstacle to achieving financial freedom.

From credit card bills to student loans, interest payments can take a considerable chunk out of your income. To manage debt, prioritize paying off high-interest debts first while making minimum payments on the lower interest ones.

10.6. Investing for Growth

This is where you set your money to work for you. From stock markets, bonds, real estate to mutual funds, your investments can provide passive income and thus get you closer to your financial freedom.

Getting a solid understanding of different investment options, along with their associated risks, is crucial before stepping into investing. Consider diversification to mitigate risks. Investing in line with your risk appetite and financial goals will be key to your roadmap.

10.7. Automating Finances

Automation can be a great tool in managing your finances. Regular aspects such as bill payments, savings, debt repayments, and investments can be automated. This not only saves time and ensures consistency but also eliminates the risk of missed payments.

10.8. Continual Learning & Adapting

Your financial journey isn't a 'set it and forget it' deal. Regular financial check-ins are necessary to assess your progress, celebrate victories, and adjust your approach if needed.

Financial freedom is not an overnight achievement but rather a consistent, disciplined approach to managing your finances over time. Take control of your financial destiny today, take that first step, and start creating your roadmap towards achieving financial freedom.

Chapter 11. Maintaining Your Financial Health Long-Term

Most individuals aim to achieve robust physical health, but maintaining your financial health often lands in the backseat, if it's considered at all. Financial health isn't just about having money in the bank but keeping a dynamic balance between income, expenses, retirement contributions, and future financial goals. Keeping your financial health intact long-term involves good financial practices, informed decision-making, and recognizing the importance of saving for the future.

11.1. Understanding Your Financial Health

The financial health of an individual doesn't transmute overnight. It's the culmination of years of financial habits. Understanding the state of your financial health involves a holistic assessment, similar to an annual physical health check-up.

1. Assess Your Debt: Determine your current debt status. Add up everything you owe. This could include car loans, student loans, mortgages, credit card debt, or medical bills.

2. Calculate Your Net worth: Net worth is the difference between your total assets (things you own) and your total liabilities (things you owe). Assets include savings account balance, retirement funds, real estate properties, stocks, cars, etc. Liabilities include any debts such as mortgages, credit card debt, and student loans.

3. Monitor Your Cash Flow: Cash flow is a calculation of your total income minus your total expenses. This includes paychecks, bill payments, rent, groceries, and leisure spending. Understanding your cash flow can highlight where your hard-earned cash is

going every month.

Reviewing these three areas will give you an approximation of your financial health. The goal is not to be discouraged by the state of your finances but to acquire a proper perspective on what needs changing or adjusting.

11.2. Building an Emergency Fund

An emergency fund should be a vital part of everyone's financial plan. This fund serves as your financial safety net. The primary purpose of this fund is to cover unexpected expenses without needing to dip into your savings or take on debt.

1. Save 3-6 Months of Expenses: A reasonable emergency fund is sufficient to provide for 3-6 months of living expenses. Start with a small, manageable amount each month and gradually increase it as you can.

2. Keep the Fund Accessible: The emergency fund should be stored in a liquid account, such as a high-yield savings account, for easy access without penalty. This fund is not an investment; it's insurance against life's unpredictable mishaps.

3. Replenish Used Funds: If you dip into your emergency fund, prioritize replenishing it as soon as possible. Treat this fund like an expense. Aim to keep it fully stocked at all times.

11.3. Overcoming The Burden of Debt

Debt can hinder financial growth and thus, needs a strategic plan for timely repayment.

1. Prioritize High-Interest Debt: Begin by paying off high-interest debt such as credit card debts. The faster these debts are cleared,

the more money you'll save in the long run.

2. Utilize the Debt Snowball Method: Pay off your debts in order of smallest to largest. Once the smallest debt is paid off, the payment that was used for that debt is now used to pay off the next smallest debt, creating a 'snowball' effect.

3. Consider Debt Consolidation: This can be a helpful tool for individuals with multiple high-interest debts. Debt consolidation merges all debts into one single debt with a lower interest rate.

11.4. Balancing Spending, Saving, and Investing

This balance may differ for everyone, but the principle remains the same: spend wisely, save diligently, and invest smartly.

1. Create and Stick to a Budget: Identify your monthly income and expenses, then create a reasonable budget that allows for savings and investments.

2. Implement the 50/30/20 Rule: Allocate 50% of your income to needs, 30% to wants, and 20% to savings and investments.

3. Utilize Automatic Transfers: Set up automatic transfers to your saving and investment accounts. This "out-of-sight, out-of-mind" method can reduce the temptation to spend that money.

Finally, while accumulating wealth, remember that frugality does not equate to deprivation. Enjoy your financial journey by creating room for spending on things you truly value and derive happiness from, while still focusing on your long-term financial health.

www.ingramcontent.com/pod-product-compliance
Lightning Source LLC
Chambersburg PA
CBHW072222290526
45794CB00007B/2844